American Moments

ABDO
&Daughters

THE LINCOLN–
DOUGLAS DEBATES

By Alan Pierce

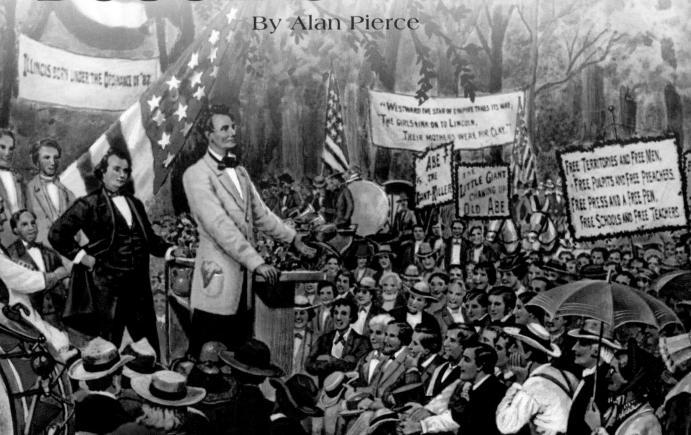

VISIT US AT
WWW.ABDOPUB.COM

Published by ABDO Publishing Company, 4940 Viking Drive, Suite 622, Edina, Minnesota 55435. Copyright © 2005 by Abdo Consulting Group, Inc. International copyrights reserved in all countries. No part of this book may be reproduced in any form without written permission from the publisher. ABDO & Daughters™ is a trademark and logo of ABDO Publishing Company.

Printed in the United States.

Edited by: Melanie A. Howard
Interior Production and Design: Terry Dunham Incorporated
Cover Design: Mighty Media
Photos: Corbis, Library of Congress, Northwind Pictures

Library of Congress Cataloging-in-Publication Data

Pierce, Alan, 1966-
  The Lincoln-Douglas debates / Alan Pierce.
    p. cm. -- (American moments)
  Includes index.
  ISBN 1-59197-734-7
  1. Lincoln-Douglas debates, 1858--Juvenile literature 2. Lincoln, Abraham, 1809-1865--Juvenile literature. 3. Douglas, Stephen Arnold, 1813-1861--Juvenile literature. I. Title. II. Series.

E457.4.P54 2005
326'.0973--dc22

2004057650

CONTENTS

THE GREAT DEBATE

On August 21, 1858, thousands of people streamed into Ottawa, Illinois. They arrived by train and by oxcart. Traffic was so heavy that dust rose from the dirt roads and formed a cloud over the town. Marching bands paraded through the streets, and flags and banners appeared throughout Ottawa.

The cause of this excitement was a debate between Abraham Lincoln and Stephen A. Douglas. Both men were running for U.S. Senate in Illinois. Douglas was the candidate from the Democratic Party. He was running for reelection to a Senate seat he had held since 1846. Lincoln was the challenger from the new Republican Party.

Douglas and Lincoln were divided over the issue of slavery. Lincoln hated slavery and wanted to see it banned from new U.S. territories. On the other hand, Douglas had helped make the spread of slavery possible.

The disagreement between Lincoln and Douglas reflected a conflict that had raged throughout the United States. For decades, politicians and other U.S. citizens had feuded about slavery. By 1858, Northern states had abolished slavery, but Southern states still used slaves. Slavery supporters and opponents disputed whether slavery should be allowed in the new territories.

Lincoln often attacked slavery in the debates with Stephen Douglas.

In Ottawa, Douglas raised the fear of war. He claimed that if Lincoln and the Republicans halted the spread of slavery, then the United States would break apart. Douglas said, "They are trying to array all the Northern States in one body against the South, to excite a sectional war between the free states and the slave states, in order that one or the other may be driven to the wall."

Douglas proved to be right about war. By 1861, the debate over slavery had ended in the United States. Eleven Southern states left the Union, and the question about slavery was settled on the battlefield.

SLAVERY

The slavery issue had tormented the nation long before Lincoln and Douglas debated in 1858. In the seventeenth century, England and other European countries transported Africans to North and South America. These Africans were forced to work in colonies established by the Europeans. Slavery took hold in the Chesapeake Bay area, where slaves worked on tobacco plantations.

In the 1660s, slavery became a legally defined institution in the English colonies of Virginia and Maryland. These colonies and others adopted laws called slave codes to control and define slavery. Under the codes, slaves were considered property. These laws also restricted the movements of slaves and imposed harsh punishments. For example, in South Carolina, slaves could be executed for destroying grain.

Slavery existed in all 13 American colonies. In South Carolina, slaves outnumbered white colonists. Slavery also thrived farther north in New York and Massachusetts. In fact, slaves made up about 30 percent of the workers in New York City in the middle of the eighteenth century.

In 1775, the American colonies rebelled against English rule. Thousands of free blacks and slaves helped the colonists in the Revolutionary War. The war ended with an American victory in 1783. But the new United States did not end slavery, despite the contributions of blacks toward American freedom.

Most slaves in the lower South worked on cotton plantations.

At this time, more people began to believe that slavery was wrong. One major reason for this growing opposition was religion. Some people felt that slavery was unchristian. The Quakers in Pennsylvania were strong opponents of slavery. Their influence was one reason that Pennsylvania became one of the first colonies to work toward abolishing slavery in 1780.

Many in the United States did not want slavery to spread beyond the original 13 colonies. In 1787, the country prohibited slavery in the Northwest Territory. This territory made up the present-day states of Ohio, Indiana, Illinois, Michigan, Wisconsin, and part of

Minnesota. On the other hand, slavery existed in the new states of Kentucky and Tennessee.

Meanwhile, there was a growing divide in the nation. By 1804, all the Northern states had abolished slavery. But slavery continued to thrive in Southern states. The major reason for this was cotton. This crop was grown in the South and slaves were used to plant and harvest it. In 1793, the invention of the cotton gin made cotton more profitable. Consequently, the demand for slaves increased.

Slaves endured a harsh life. Many toiled as long as 15 hours a day. In addition, slaves often faced physical punishment such as whippings. Abuse was common. This fact was evident in advertisements of runaway slaves. Often, the advertisements included descriptions of scars and other injuries that slaves had suffered from punishment.

Another terrible prospect was a fact of life for some slaves. Owners sometimes broke up families by selling slaves. In other cases, owners rented out slaves to other people. These slaves might be separated from their families for years.

Slavery eventually spread, despite efforts to contain it. In 1803, the United States purchased the Louisiana Territory from France. This 828,000-square-mile (2,144,520-sq-km) region between the Mississippi River and Rocky Mountains became known as the Louisiana Purchase. Several territories were eventually formed from this area, including the Missouri Territory. By 1817, Missouri wanted to be admitted as a slave state.

Congress fought over whether to admit Missouri as a slave state or a free state. Finally, a compromise was reached in 1820. Missouri would be admitted as a slave state and Maine would join the Union as a free state. The agreement also banned slavery in the Louisiana

A poster announces a reward for an escaped slave.

Territory north of Missouri's southern border. This settlement became known as the Missouri Compromise. Many hoped it would settle the dispute over slavery in the territories.

Americans continued to have strong feelings about slavery. In the South, slavery grew because slaves were valuable. They became an investment like land or railroads. Also, ownership of slaves became a symbol of social importance.

In the North, opposition to slavery increased. People dedicated to ending slavery were known as abolitionists. In December 1833, many abolitionists met in Philadelphia, Pennsylvania. They formed the American Anti-Slavery Society. Members of the group called for the immediate end of slavery. Within the next few years, the society had gained more than 150,000 members.

ABRAHAM LINCOLN

During this time of growing antislavery activity, Abraham Lincoln worked as a store clerk in New Salem, Illinois. In 1832, he ran for a seat in the Illinois legislature as a candidate for the Whig Party. This new party supported a plan for the federal government to build roads and canals. Lincoln believed that Illinois could benefit from these projects.

However, a military conflict interrupted Lincoln's campaign. Sauk and Fox Native Americans had recently been forced from Illinois into what is now Iowa. In 1832, their leader, Black Hawk, brought about 1,000 followers back to Illinois to plant crops.

Fighting broke out in the Black Hawk War between the Native Americans and the Illinois militia. Lincoln joined the militia and was elected captain of his group. He served a few months, but did not take part in any fighting. By August, the Native Americans were defeated.

Lincoln lost the election in 1832. However, in 1834, he ran again and was elected as a representative to the Illinois legislature. At this time, the Illinois state capital was in Vandalia. Lincoln lived in this town with other lawmakers while the legislature was in session. In Vandalia, Lincoln saw Stephen A. Douglas for the first time. Douglas had recently been elected to the state legislature as a Democrat.

Lincoln also began to take a serious interest in studying law. His friend John Todd Stuart had encouraged Lincoln to become a lawyer.

YOUNG LINCOLN

On February 12, 1809, Abraham Lincoln was born in a log cabin near Hodgenville, Kentucky. His parents were Thomas and Nancy Lincoln, and he also had an older sister named Sarah. A younger brother, Thomas, died in infancy.

When he was seven, Lincoln's family moved to Pigeon Creek, Indiana. Nancy Lincoln died from an illness by late 1818. Thomas Lincoln remarried the next year. His new wife was Sarah Bush Johnston Lincoln. She made sure that Lincoln received enough education to read and write. It was enough to inspire an interest in reading.

Lincoln was a devoted reader.

The Lincoln family moved to Illinois in 1830. At about this time, Lincoln first worked on a riverboat. He shuttled cargo down the Mississippi River to New Orleans, Louisiana.

It is said that Lincoln grew to believe that slavery was wrong from seeing slaves at auction during this journey. Other sources say that Lincoln's opinions about slavery formed even earlier. Lincoln once said, "I am naturally antislavery. If slavery is not wrong, nothing is wrong. I can not remember when I did not so think, and feel."

After the legislature adjourned, Lincoln studied law books and applied for a license to practice law. He received his license in 1836.

Lincoln won reelection to the state legislature that same year. He and other legislators planned to move the state capital. They wanted to relocate the capital from Vandalia to the larger town of Springfield. In 1837, they succeeded in making Springfield the new state capital. About this time, Lincoln moved to Springfield to practice law.

Issues besides the location of the state capital also concerned Lincoln. In 1837, the legislature considered resolutions condemning the efforts of abolitionists. Lincoln and another legislator, Dan Stone, refused to support it. They wrote that slavery was "founded on both injustice and bad policy ... " However, in order to satisfy some voters, Lincoln also refused to approve of abolitionists.

Lincoln was reelected in 1838 and 1840. But the Whig Party did not nominate him to run for office again. By 1841, Lincoln had lost interest in state politics. He had entered the legislature with hopes of backing road, canal, and railroad construction in Illinois. However, these projects proved too costly and were never fulfilled.

At this time, Lincoln courted a woman named Mary Todd. She had grown up in Kentucky but had moved to Springfield. There, she lived with her sister, Elizabeth Edwards, and her sister's husband, Ninian. On November 4, 1842, Lincoln and Mary Todd were married. In 1843, their first son, Robert Todd, was born. A second son, Edward Baker, was born in 1846.

Mary Todd Lincoln

In the Mexican War, U.S. and Mexican forces battled beneath the fortress of Chapultepec. U.S. soldiers captured the fortress on September 13, 1847.

Lincoln also returned to politics. But this time he ran for a seat in the U.S. Congress, and not the Illinois legislature. In 1846, he became a Whig congressional candidate. He won his seat in the House of Representatives by defeating Democrat Peter Cartwright.

Lincoln became a U.S. representative during a time of immense national change. Tensions had increased between Mexico and the United States. Much of this hostility concerned disputes over land. Texas had gained its independence from Mexico in 1836. The Mexican government was further angered when the United States annexed Texas in 1845. At this time, New Mexico and California were part of Mexico. The United States wanted to acquire these territories, also.

In April 1846, a clash between Mexican and U.S. forces near the Rio Grande led to war between the two countries. U.S. president

James K. Polk declared that Mexican soldiers had attacked American troops on U.S. soil. Congressman Lincoln opposed the war. He challenged the president to prove that the attack had occurred on U.S. territory. The border between the two countries was still unsettled, Lincoln pointed out.

The Mexican War opened up another dispute about slavery. U.S. representative David Wilmot of Pennsylvania proposed an amendment that would ban slavery in territory acquired from Mexico. Lincoln supported the amendment, which became known as the Wilmot Proviso. The amendment provoked bitter debates between Northerners and Southerners, and it never became law.

The issue raised by Wilmot was important because the United States acquired a vast amount of territory from Mexico. The war ended with a U.S. victory in 1848. As part of the Treaty of Guadalupe Hidalgo, Mexico ceded land that would become all or part of several states. These states include California, New Mexico, Utah, Nevada, Arizona, Colorado, and Texas.

Lincoln was also concerned about slavery in Washington DC. In 1849, he announced that he was working on a bill to abolish slavery in the District of Columbia. Under Lincoln's plan, slave owners would be compensated for their

The United States acquired 500,000 square miles (1.3 million sq km) of land from Mexico in the Mexican War.

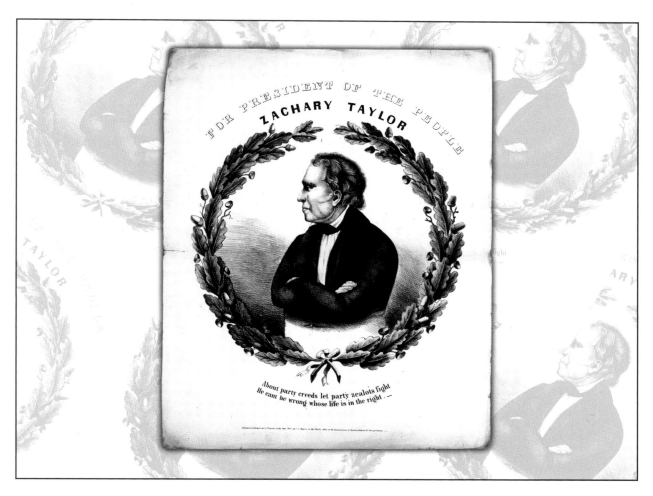

In 1848, the Whig Party nominated Zachary Taylor to run for president.

slaves. But Lincoln's plan never received much support. Both Southerners and abolitionists criticized the proposal. Lincoln gave up on the bill.

Lincoln later worked for Zachary Taylor's presidential campaign. Taylor was a hero of the Mexican War, and was the Whig candidate for president. After Taylor won, Lincoln hoped the new president would appoint him commissioner of the general land office. Instead, Lincoln was offered the position of governor of the Oregon Territory. He did not want the job. He was disappointed, and left Congress after serving one term. Lincoln returned to Springfield to continue practicing law.

THE LITTLE GIANT

Stephen A. Douglas entered politics in Illinois at about the same time that Abraham Lincoln did. Unlike Lincoln, Douglas was not a member of the Whig Party. Instead, Douglas was a strong supporter of Democratic president Andrew Jackson. In fact, Douglas's enthusiastic speeches for Jackson helped earn Douglas the nickname "Little Giant." Douglas stood five feet four (1.6 m), but he was a powerful speaker.

While in his 20s, Douglas held a number of political posts. In 1835, he was elected to serve as a prosecutor for a circuit court. The next year, he won a seat in the Illinois House of Representatives. He also ran unsuccessfully for a seat in the U.S. Congress in 1838. Three years later, he served as a justice in the Illinois Supreme Court. Douglas remained there until he was elected to the U.S. House of Representatives in 1842.

Douglas served in the House until he was elected to the U.S. Senate in 1846. In the Senate, he served as chairman of the Senate Committee on Territories. This committee made important decisions for the territories such as setting up post offices, courts, and legislatures. However, slavery was a different matter. Douglas wanted to adopt a policy that was acceptable to both Northerners and Southerners.

A YOUNG POLITICIAN

Stephen Arnold Douglass was born on April 23, 1813, in Brandon, Vermont. He later began writing his last name as Douglas. When he was two months old, Douglas's father, also named Stephen Arnold, died unexpectedly. His mother, Sarah Fiske Douglas, and his uncle raised him.

In his youth, Douglas worked with a cabinetmaker. But his real interest was politics. At the age of 15, Douglas was already a dedicated follower of presidential candidate Andrew Jackson.

In 1830, Douglas moved with his mother and her new husband, Gehazi Granger, to New York. Douglas attended Canandaigua Academy there that year. But then he decided to go west to make his own fortune.

Douglas spent time in Cleveland, Ohio, and St. Louis, Missouri. He then settled in Jacksonville, Illinois, to study law. For a while, he ran a school. But at the age of 20, he became a lawyer and opened an office in Jacksonville. He then began working on his political career.

Stephen Douglas

To settle the matter of slavery in the territories, Douglas used an idea known as popular sovereignty. This viewpoint maintained that people living in the territories should decide the slavery issue for themselves. But not everyone supported this policy. People in New England especially disliked popular sovereignty.

The Compromise of 1850

By 1849, the United States faced a worsening crisis over slavery. In December, the territory of California wished to join the Union as a free state. California's request for admission fueled the bitterness between supporters and opponents of slavery in Congress. The United States still had not answered the question of how to address slavery in the territories acquired from Mexico.

In January 1850, Senator Henry Clay of Kentucky proposed solutions to this problem and other issues. California would be admitted as a free state. The slave trade would be ended in the District of Columbia. However, laws would be strengthened to help slave owners recover escaped slaves. Also, Utah and New Mexico would be organized into territories. But these territories would not be identified as either slave or free. Popular sovereignty would be tried in Utah and New Mexico.

Poor health prevented Clay from fighting for his bills. Douglas stepped in to pilot Clay's legislation through Congress. He managed to get most of Clay's bills passed through the Senate. By September, Clay's bills had become enacted into law. These laws became known as the Compromise of 1850.

Many Americans hoped the compromise would preserve the Union. But some people in the South were unhappy with the compromise.

Some Southerners had held a convention in Nashville, Tennessee, in June. They had discussed ways to respond to what they felt was a hostile North. Later, they condemned the Compromise of 1850. They also called for Southern states to leave the Union. However, their demand to secede received little support in the South.

In the North, people were angry about the compromise because it included the Fugitive Slave Act of 1850. This law helped slave owners regain slaves who had escaped to other states or territories. It imposed fines and jail sentences on anyone who rescued or hid runaway slaves. The harsher penalties failed to work. Abolitionists increased their efforts to help slaves escape to freedom.

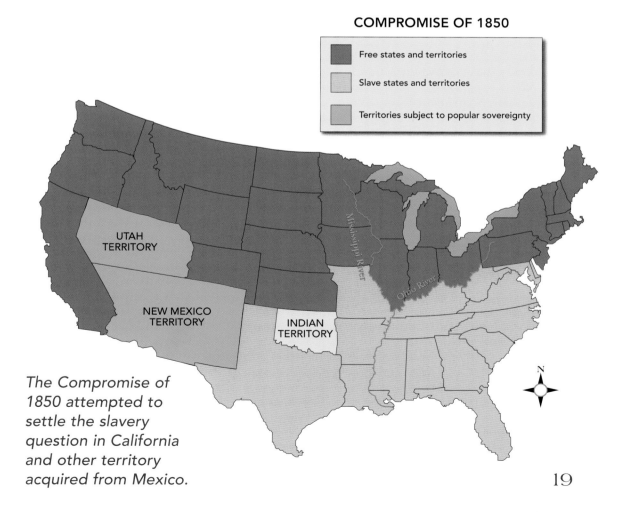

COMPROMISE OF 1850

Free states and territories

Slave states and territories

Territories subject to popular sovereignty

The Compromise of 1850 attempted to settle the slavery question in California and other territory acquired from Mexico.

BATTLES OVER SLAVERY

In 1854, another crisis over slavery emerged. Douglas presented a bill in Congress to form two territories from the Nebraska Territory. These two new territories would be called Nebraska and Kansas. Douglas also applied the idea of popular sovereignty to these two regions.

Douglas's act voided the Missouri Compromise, which had banned slavery north of Missouri's southern border. It created the possibility that slavery might be permitted in areas where it had been prohibited. Opponents of slavery were angry about Douglas's plan. Nevertheless, the Kansas-Nebraska Act became law on May 30, 1854.

The act upset Lincoln. He hated the possibility that slavery might be extended west. He attacked the Kansas-Nebraska Act in a speech in Peoria, Illinois. Lincoln ran for U.S. Senate so that he could oppose the spread of slavery. However, he lost the election in February 1855.

Meanwhile, popular sovereignty had become a disaster for Kansas. Antislavery Northerners and proslavery Southerners swarmed into the territory. Each group set up its own legislature. The dispute over slavery slid into violence. On May 21, 1856, slavery supporters attacked the town of Lawrence. The town was considered a site for antislavery activity. A few days later, abolitionist John Brown's gang

JOHN BROWN

John Brown was born on May 9, 1800, in Torrington, Connecticut. He was a strong abolitionist all his life, and so were some of his sons. Five of Brown's sons moved to Kansas after the passage of the Kansas-Nebraska Act in 1854. Brown followed them there in 1855, and settled near Osawatomie.

Brown led attacks against proslavery settlers in Kansas in 1856. Later, he left Kansas to initiate an ambitious plan. On October 16, 1859, he and several abolitionists took over the armory at Harpers Ferry in present-day West Virginia. They hoped to establish an army to liberate slaves in the South.

On the morning of October 18, federal troops overwhelmed the abolitionists. Several people were killed, including two of Brown's sons. Brown was captured, and was brought to trial later that month. He was convicted of treason, conspiracy, and murder. On December 2, Brown was hanged.

John Brown

killed five slavery supporters. These events helped the territory earn the name Bleeding Kansas.

Anger over the Kansas-Nebraska Act remained strong. Some of those who despised the act and slavery formed a new political party in 1854. It was called the Republican Party. Republicans believed that Congress should abolish slavery in the territories.

Lincoln had been searching for another party to join. The Whig Party had split between supporters and opponents of slavery.

Dred Scott

Roger B. Taney

It became apparent that, to fight against slavery, he should join the new Republican Party. In 1856, he did so.

Soon, one man's legal struggle for freedom upset the discussion about slavery. A slave named Dred Scott had lived with his owner, Dr. John Emerson, in Missouri, as well as in Illinois and the Wisconsin Territory. Slavery was banned both in Illinois and Wisconsin. When Scott was in Missouri, he sued for his freedom in 1846. Scott's lawsuit was based on the fact that he had lived in free areas. A circuit court ruled in favor of Scott's freedom. But the Missouri Supreme Court overturned the circuit court's decision.

The U.S. Supreme Court considered Scott's lawsuit. On March 6, 1857, the court made its ruling. The nine justices voted 7-2 to refuse

Scott's demand for freedom. Chief Justice Roger B. Taney wrote that blacks were not U.S. citizens. Therefore, they could not file suits in federal court.

Taney also addressed the issue of slavery in the territories. He wrote that the Missouri Compromise was unconstitutional. Congress lacked the power to forbid slavery in the territories. As a result, Scott's residence in the Wisconsin Territory did not make him free. Most of the justices also ruled that Scott's residence in Illinois did not make him free, either. The Court ruled that slaves were property and slave owners had a constitutional right to their property.

The Dred Scott case inflamed the debate about slavery. Southerners were pleased with the Supreme Court's ruling. In contrast, many people in the North detested the decision. Some leaders even wondered whether they should accept the Court's ruling. The case also disheartened free blacks. Many believed there was no future for them in the United States.

Republicans were upset because the ruling spoiled the party's goal to block the expansion of slavery. Many feared that the decision was part of a conspiracy by slave owners to spread slavery throughout the country. Republicans condemned the court's decision.

The Supreme Court decision alarmed Douglas. He realized that the Court had hurt popular sovereignty. The Court had ruled that Congress had no power to bar slavery from the territories. Consequently, the weaker territorial legislatures also had no power to ban slavery. In June 1857, Douglas addressed the issue of popular sovereignty in a speech in Springfield. He insisted that slavery could still be prohibited in the territories. They could do this by refusing to pass laws that would give police the power to enforce slavery.

A HOUSE DIVIDED

The problem of slavery in the territories became more urgent. In 1857, the Kansas Territory requested to become a state, but this process was plagued with controversy. Kansas residents were supposed to vote on a constitution that allowed slavery and one that prohibited slavery. In reality, they were not given a choice. Slavery supporters had written a constitution in Lecompton, Kansas, that would permit slavery no matter how people voted.

In February 1858, Congress considered the Lecompton Constitution and Kansas's request to become a state. The Lecompton Constitution would make Kansas a slave state. Douglas opposed the Lecompton Constitution. He believed it violated the principle of popular sovereignty. People in Kansas never received a real chance to vote on slavery, Douglas believed. Although the Senate accepted the Lecompton Constitution, the House rejected it.

Douglas's opposition to the Lecompton Constitution made him popular with some Republicans in Illinois. This situation upset Lincoln. He did not want Douglas to influence the Republican Party. Lincoln wished to challenge Douglas for the U.S. Senate seat.

On June 16, 1858, Illinois Republicans nominated Lincoln to run against Douglas. At the party's convention in Springfield, Illinois, Lincoln accepted the nomination. In a speech to the convention,

LINCOLN'S LANGUAGE

Abraham Lincoln's speeches are considered some of the greatest contributions to the English language. Despite this, some have debated whether or not he was a great orator. Lincoln spoke with a plain and direct style. Some point to other speakers of the nineteenth century, most notably U.S. Senators Daniel Webster and John C. Calhoun, as better examples of great orators.

Lincoln used language from the Bible to compare the United States to a house. Lincoln said, "'A house divided against itself cannot stand.' I believe this government cannot endure, permanently, half slave and half free. I do not expect the Union to be dissolved; I do not expect the house to fall; but I do expect it will cease to be divided. It will become all one thing, or all the other. Either the opponents of slavery will arrest the further spread of it and place it where the public mind shall rest in the belief that it is in the course of ultimate extinction, or its advocates will push it forward till it shall become alike lawful in all the states, old as well as new, North as well as South."

Republicans at the convention were thrilled with the address, which became known as the "House Divided" speech. But other Republicans believed that Lincoln had sounded too threatening.

They thought that Lincoln intended to fight a war over slavery. Douglas also accused Lincoln of promoting war. Lincoln denied this.

Some of Lincoln's advisers believed he should debate Douglas. A debate might allow Lincoln's campaign to recover from the controversy of his speech. In July, he challenged Douglas to 50 debates.

Douglas did not wish to debate. The debates would likely help Lincoln, who was less well-known than Douglas. However, Douglas agreed to debate. He liked the idea of facing Lincoln.

Instead of 50 debates, however, Douglas suggested 7. The debates would occur in the 7 congressional districts of Illinois where both candidates had not already spoken.

Douglas also proposed the form for the debates. The first candidate would speak for one hour. Then the other man would speak for an hour and a half. Next, the first candidate would have a half hour to respond. Douglas's proposal called for him to speak first and last in four of the seven debates. Lincoln agreed to Douglas's terms.

The two candidates had agreed to debate before crowds throughout Illinois. But the registered voters would not elect Lincoln or Douglas to the Senate. At this time, state legislators elected U.S. senators. When Lincoln and Douglas debated, they were campaigning for state legislative candidates who would vote for them.

The campaign also had attracted attention outside of Illinois. Speeches made by Lincoln and Douglas appeared in newspapers in the eastern United States. Also, Douglas was considered a serious presidential candidate. Consequently, interest in the debates was high throughout the country. When Lincoln and Douglas spoke, they addressed millions of people in the United States.

Opposite page: *Map showing locations and dates of the Lincoln-Douglas debates*

Lake Michigan

IOWA

★
2. Freeport
August 27

★
1. Ottawa
August 21

★
5. Galesburg
October 7

ILLINOIS

INDIANA

★
6. Quincy
October 13

★
4. Charleston
September 18

★
7. Alton
October 15

★
3. Jonesboro
September 15

MISSOURI

KENTUCKY

N

OTTAWA

In Ottawa, Lincoln and Douglas appeared on a platform in the town's square. The audience could see the contrast between the two men. Lincoln stood six feet four (1.9 m) while Douglas was a foot (30.5 cm) shorter. The men also exhibited a different speaking style. Douglas had a deep voice and spoke fast. Lincoln spoke with a high-pitched voice that could be heard far away.

Their differences were more than physical. They stressed their disagreements about the nation's policy toward slavery. Douglas attacked Lincoln's "House Divided" speech. The nation could exist half free and half slave, Douglas insisted. In fact, the nation's founders had established the country that way.

Douglas also defended popular sovereignty. He said, "I hold that New York had as much right to abolish slavery as Virginia has to continue it, and that each and every State of this Union is a sovereign power, with the right to do as it pleases upon this question of slavery, and upon all its domestic institutions."

Douglas also spoke about the position of blacks in U.S. society. Blacks were not equal to whites, Douglas said. In addition, Douglas opposed citizenship for blacks. He said he would not allow free blacks to vote in Illinois even though they had that right in other states.

In this cartoon, Douglas is portrayed as a political hero armed with weapons such as popular sovereignty and majority rule.

Lincoln disagreed with Douglas. The nation's founders had intended for slavery to die out, Lincoln declared. They had taken steps to make sure that slavery did not spread. Early in the nation's history, the founders had restricted slavery from the territories. They had also halted the country's involvement in the slave trade.

Popular sovereignty was no cure for the slavery issue, Lincoln said. People had lost their right to oppose slavery. The Supreme Court had made it impossible to keep slavery from spreading to the territories. Lincoln said, " ... as I understand the Dred Scott decision, if any one man wants slaves, all the rest have no way of keeping that one man from holding them."

Lincoln also stood up for the rights of blacks. He said " ... there is no reason in the world why the Negro is not entitled to all the natural rights enumerated in the Declaration of Independence, the right to life, liberty, and the pursuit of happiness. I hold that he is as much entitled to these as the white man."

For Lincoln, the most important issue was the evil of slavery. Lincoln attacked Douglas for allowing slavery to spread. "When he invites any people, willing to have slavery, to establish it, he is blowing out the moral lights around us," Lincoln said.

Still, Lincoln shared some of the racist views of his time. He said in some ways blacks were not equal to whites. And although Lincoln hated slavery, he did not want to end it in states where it already existed. "I believe I have no lawful right to do so, and I have no inclination to do so," he said.

Opposite page: *Lincoln delivers a speech during the Lincoln-Douglas debates. Douglas stands behind him.*

FREEPORT DOCTRINE

On August 27, the two candidates met in Freeport. More than 13,000 people gathered for the debate. The same festive feeling that had prevailed in Ottawa was also widespread in Freeport. Marching bands played and banners hung in the town.

For this debate, Lincoln questioned Douglas about popular sovereignty. Lincoln planned to ask Douglas how popular sovereignty could work after the Dred Scott decision. The Supreme Court had ruled that slavery could not be barred from the territories. Yet, popular sovereignty maintained that people in the territories had a choice about slavery.

Speaking first, Lincoln asked Douglas whether people in a territory could ban slavery before they adopted a state constitution. Douglas told Lincoln that he had answered this question in many other speeches. He said people in a territory could exclude slavery by failing to enact slave codes. Slavery could not exist in a territory unless it was protected by these codes, Douglas argued.

Douglas's solution became known as the Freeport Doctrine. It was one of the most important factors to emerge from the debates. People throughout the United States became aware of Douglas's desire to preserve popular sovereignty. His solution made Douglas far less popular among slave supporters in the South. This would

A poster announces a reenactment of a Lincoln-Douglas debate. The performance took place the same day Lincoln and Douglas debated in Freeport, Illinois.

not matter in the Senate race in Illinois. However, this loss of support in the South would hurt Douglas in a presidential election.

After Freeport, Lincoln and Douglas continued the debates. The debate in Jonesboro attracted less than 1,500 people. Neither candidate had much support in this part of the state. Rain also kept many away.

In Jonesboro, Lincoln attacked the Freeport Doctrine. He said that slavery could exist in territories where slave codes did not exist. Dred Scott was an example of this situation. Scott had lived as a slave in a free territory. "This shows that there is vigor enough in slavery to plant itself in a new country even against unfriendly legislation," Lincoln said.

Douglas disagreed. He insisted that the Freeport Doctrine was still workable. "We come right back, therefore, to the practical question, if the people of a territory want slavery they will have it, and if they do not want it you cannot force it on them," Douglas said.

In the remaining debates, the candidates continued to stress their points. Douglas defended popular sovereignty. He also repeated his belief that blacks were not equal to whites. Lincoln persisted in attacking slavery.

On November 2, Illinois voters went to the polls to elect state legislators. These legislators, in turn, would elect either Douglas or Lincoln to the U.S. Senate. Republican candidates received 125,000 votes to 121,000 votes cast for Democrats who supported Douglas. However, these vote totals did not mean that Lincoln had won. Republican votes were not distributed evenly in the state. As a result, more Democrats won election to the state legislature.

On January 5, 1859, the Illinois legislature reelected Douglas to the U.S. Senate. Douglas won the election by a vote of 54 to 46. Lincoln felt disappointed. But he was proud that he had fought against slavery.

Opposite page: One of the debates took place at Knox College in Galesburg, Illinois. There, Lincoln had a lot of support.

DEFEAT AND VICTORY

Lincoln had campaigned hard against Douglas. Although Lincoln had lost the election, many people had been impressed with him in the debates. He received invitations to give speeches. Some Illinois newspapers suggested Lincoln as a presidential candidate. He had also gained the attention of Republicans in the eastern United States.

The debate had helped Lincoln in another way. Republicans had urged the publication of the debates in book form. This book sold about 100,000 copies, and it strengthened Lincoln's position as a Republican leader.

Douglas, however, was hurt by the debates. Southerners were angry with Douglas about the Freeport Doctrine. They did not trust him to defend the expansion of slavery. Douglas's political enemies weakened his power by removing him from serving as chairman of the territories committee.

At the Democratic convention in Baltimore, Maryland, delegates nominated Douglas for their presidential candidate. But the South's anger toward Douglas harmed him in the 1860 presidential election. A group of Southern Democrats broke away to nominate a different candidate. They chose John C. Breckinridge, who was serving as vice president of the United States. Breckinridge believed that slavery should not be barred from the territories.

LINCOLN'S FIRST VICE PRESIDENT

In 1860, the Republican National Committee nominated Hannibal Hamlin to run for vice president alongside Lincoln. Hamlin had started his political career as a Jacksonian Democrat like Stephen Douglas. However, Hamlin had left the Democratic Party because of his antislavery beliefs in 1856. Republicans believed that because Hamlin was a former Democrat, he would be a good balance for Lincoln. Instead, he was dropped from the presidential ticket in 1864 because of his ties to the Radical Republicans.

Still, another political party offered voters a choice. The Constitutional Union Party avoided the issue of slavery. Instead, it tried to unite Americans in support of the Union and the Constitution. This party drew most of its support from people in slave states bordering on the North. The party nominated John Bell to run for president. Bell was a former U.S. senator from Tennessee and a slave owner.

The Republicans were more united than the Democrats. In May 1860, delegates met at the Republican National Convention in Chicago, Illinois. They nominated Lincoln, who encouraged harmony among Republicans. Lincoln's efforts were successful. On November 6, 1860, he won the presidential election. Lincoln received the electoral votes from the free states. The slave states split their electoral votes among Breckinridge, Bell, and Douglas.

Lincoln's election helped bring on a national crisis. By December, South Carolina had voted to secede from the Union. Moreover, South Carolina asked other slave states to form a confederacy. Mississippi, Florida, Alabama, Georgia, Louisiana, and Texas left the Union. These states became the first confederate states to join South Carolina.

In the face of this emergency, Lincoln and Douglas worked together. Douglas was outraged by the decision of the Southern states to secede. Some Democrats attacked Lincoln's inaugural address for being too hostile toward the South. However, Douglas defended the address in the Senate.

As the crisis grew more serious, Douglas continued to support Lincoln. On April 12, 1861, confederate forces fired on Fort Sumter in the harbor of Charleston, South Carolina. This attack provoked the first fighting in the Civil War. Lincoln called for 75,000 troops to

Fort Sumter after its destruction

subdue the rebellion. Douglas was furious about the attack. He said he would call up 200,000 soldiers.

The president's request for troops, however, deepened the crisis. Virginia, North Carolina, Tennessee, and Arkansas seceded. The eleven states that left the Union formed the Confederate States of America.

Lincoln asked Douglas to rally support for the Union. Douglas obeyed the president's request and traveled west to give speeches. In May 1861, Douglas arrived in Chicago. He became sick with typhoid fever and died on June 3. Lincoln had lost a valuable ally in the cause to maintain the Union.

Lincoln discusses the Emancipation Proclamation with his cabinet.

Lincoln also confronted the question of slavery. On September 22, 1862, Lincoln issued the Emancipation Proclamation. This order addressed slavery in the Confederate states. Lincoln declared that if Confederate states did not return to the Union by the end of the year, then these slaves would be declared free. No states returned to the Union. Lincoln declared the final Emancipation Proclamation on January 1, 1863.

The Emancipation Proclamation had little effect on the slaves in Confederate territory. Despite the proclamation, Lincoln had no real authority to free slaves where Union armies had no control. However, the proclamation set a new tone for the war. Lincoln had declared that the war was a struggle for liberation as well as for preserving the Union.

Lincoln also worked toward real liberation for the slaves. He urged the Republican Party and Congress to support a constitutional amendment to abolish slavery. Thanks to Lincoln's efforts, Congress passed the constitutional amendment in January 1865. The states then considered the amendment for ratification. Lincoln was proud that Illinois was the first state to ratify the Thirteenth Amendment.

On April 9, 1865, the Confederate army in Virginia surrendered to Union forces. The president had led the Union to victory. But he did not live to see the Thirteenth Amendment ratified. On April 14, John Wilkes Booth assassinated Lincoln at Ford's Theatre in Washington DC. The president died the next day. Lincoln's death, however, did not prevent acceptance of the Thirteenth Amendment. It was ratified in December 1865.

Lincoln had considered the Thirteenth Amendment one of his most important acts. It destroyed a system he believed was immoral. He had opposed slavery since he was a young man. But the nation became aware of his aversion during the Lincoln-Douglas debates.

Before a crowd of 20,000 people in Galesburg, Illinois, Lincoln had declared his hatred of slavery. "Now, I confess myself as belonging to that class in the country who contemplate slavery as a moral, social and political evil ... " he said. Lincoln added that he looked "hopefully to the time when as a wrong it may come to an end." Lincoln had helped make that time come to pass.

TIMELINE

 1775 to 1783 The United States fights the Revolutionary War against Great Britain.

 1787 Slavery is prohibited in the Northwest Territory.

 1803 The United States purchases the Louisiana Territory from France.

 1820 The Missouri Compromise of 1820 admits Missouri as a slave state. However, slavery is banned from the rest of the Louisiana Territory north of Missouri's southern border.

 1846 to 1848 Mexico and the United States fight the Mexican War.

 1850 In September, Congress passes a series of laws known as the Compromise of 1850.

 1854 On May 30, Congress passes the Kansas-Nebraska Act, which supports popular sovereignty in these territories.

The Republican Party forms.

 1856 On May 21, slavery supporters attack Lawrence, Kansas. Abolitionists kill proslavery settlers. The territory earns the nickname of "Bleeding Kansas."

 1857 On March 6, the Supreme Court rules on the Dred Scott case. In its ruling, the Supreme Court states that Congress cannot ban slavery from the territories.

1858 In July, Representative Abraham Lincoln challenges Senator Stephen A. Douglas to 50 debates. Douglas agrees to 7.

On August 27, at the Freeport, Illinois, debate, Douglas announces his Freeport Doctrine.

1860 On November 6, Lincoln wins the presidential election.

1861 On April 12, Confederate forces attack Fort Sumter in Charleston, South Carolina. The Civil War begins.

On June 3, Douglas dies in Chicago, Illinois.

1862 On September 22, Lincoln announces that he will free the Confederate slaves if the Confederate states do not return to the Union. He declares these slaves free on January 1, 1863 in the Emancipation Proclamation.

1865 On April 9, the Confederate army surrenders in Virginia to Union forces, ending the Civil War.

On April 14, John Wilkes Booth assassinates Lincoln.

In December, the Thirteenth Amendment is ratified, making slavery illegal.

American Moments

FAST FACTS

Lincoln's namesake was his grandfather, Abraham Lincoln. Abraham moved from Virginia to Kentucky in 1782. In 1786, Abraham was killed in a conflict with Native Americans. Thomas Lincoln, President Lincoln's father, was Abraham's youngest son.

Three years after the death of his first wife, Martha Denny Martin, in 1853, Stephen A. Douglas married Adèle Cutts. Cutts's great aunt was Dolley Madison, the wife of former president James Madison. Dolley is famous for saving the Gilbert Stuart portrait of George Washington when the British burned the White House during the War of 1812.

Altogether, Abraham Lincoln and Mary Todd Lincoln had four children. All of them were boys. Only the eldest, Robert Todd, lived into adulthood. Edward Baker died in 1850 and was nearly four years old. William Wallace died in 1862 at the age of 11. Lincoln's youngest son, Thomas, died at the age of 18 in 1871.

Douglas's last words to his children were, "Tell them to obey the laws and support the Constitution of the United States." Similar words are engraved on his tomb in Douglas Monument Park in Chicago, Illinois.

In 1991, a letter that Abraham Lincoln wrote on January 8, 1863, was sold at an auction in New York City, New York. The letter was written to Major General John Alexander McClernand in Memphis, Tennessee. In the letter, Lincoln defended the Emancipation Proclamation. It was sold for $748,000, making it the world's most valuable letter.

WEB SITES
WWW.ABDOPUB.COM

Would you like to learn more about the Lincoln-Douglas debates? Please visit **www.abdopub.com** to find up-to-date Web site links about the Lincoln-Douglas debates and other American moments. These links are routinely monitored and updated to provide the most current information available.

Badges from Lincoln's 1864 presidential campaign

GLOSSARY

abolitionist: someone who is against slavery.

array: to arrange in a certain order.

circuit court: a state court.

conspiracy: a joining together of two or more people to commit a crime. Conspiracy is also used to describe an evil act that seems to have been planned.

Constitutional Union Party: a political party formed on May 9, 1860. The party wanted to find a peaceful solution to the slavery issue. After the 1860 election, the party broke apart, due to the coming of the Civil War.

Declaration of Independence: an essay written at the Second Continental Congress in 1776, announcing the separation of the American colonies from England.

Democratic Party: a political party that supported farmers and landowners in Lincoln's time.

domestic: of, relating to, or originating within a country.

enumerate: to list.

lawsuit: a case brought to court because of a perceived wrong.

militia: a group of citizens trained for war or emergencies.

prosecutor: a lawyer who argues to convict the person on trial.

proviso: a condition or restriction.

Quaker: a member of the religious group called the Society of Friends.

racism: a belief that one race is better than another.

Republican Party: a political party that supported business and strong government in Lincoln's time.

secede: to break away from a group.

sovereign: independent or self-governing.

typhoid: also called typhus. Typhoid is a bacterial disease spread by lice that causes fever and a dark red rash.

unconstitutional: not consistent with the Constitution.

Whig Party: a political party that was very strong in the early 1800s, but ended in the 1850s. Whigs supported laws that helped business.

INDEX